W9-BVJ-313

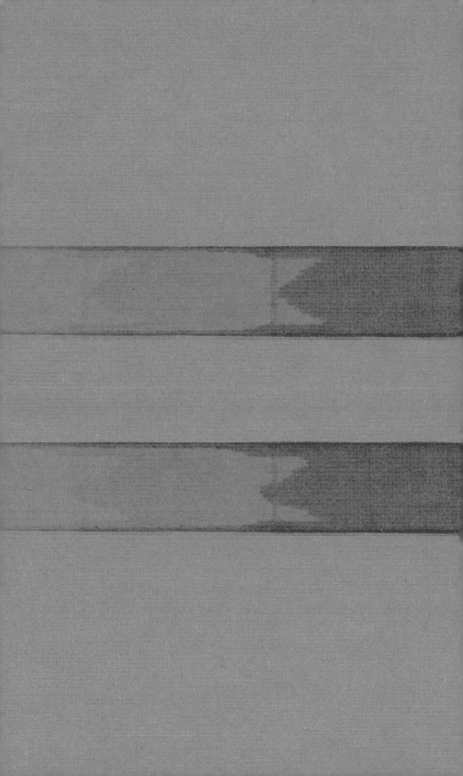

HORACE:
TWELVE
ODES

HORACE: TWELVE ODES

XII

Translated by

Leonard Moskovit

Library of Congress Catalog Card Number 83-062340
ISBN 0-937672-13-0

Cover design by Lazarillo

Rowan Tree Press
124 Chestnut Street
Boston, Massachusetts 02108

To Harriet,
my best critic

PREFACE

I'd like to explain to the reader what I try to do in these translations and what I do not try to do.

My general aim, however unpopular it may be in this age of "free" translations, paraphrases, and imitations, is to produce versions as close to the original as possible—in sense, tone, and sometimes sentence emphasis. Although every translation may be an interpretation, even a critique, of its original, yet I try to efface myself as much as I can. The reader, I am sure, is interested in Horace and the poetic experience he presents, not in me and mine.

Although Latin versification is so different from our own that it cannot even be partly duplicated, I have tried to hint at Horace's form in the sense of his line lengths, stanzas, and even the way sentence patterns string out over lines and between stanzas. I do not use rime, partly because it does not exist in classical Latin verse and partly because the search for similar English sounds leads away from the Latin meaning.

I have modernized nothing. I do not believe that Horace should be violently dragged into our age; rather, we must travel back to his. Accordingly, I do not try to make Horace sound like a modern poet who thinks that free verse and colloquial language are the only legitimate means of poetic expression.

There are, of course, difficulties in understanding the context or milieu of these Latin lyrics. Occasionally, where space permits, I add a word or two to clarify allusions and names. But I refuse to go so far in this as to interfere with the form of the poem. I hope the "arguments" will help explain the fictional situation of each poem. Those who want more information should consult two or three annotated editions of the odes in the original. The date of the edition is of no importance whatsoever.

The reader, then, may be confident that almost nothing that is in the original has been left out, and that what little has been added is only a slight expansion of what is already there.

Leonard Moskovit

HORACE:
TWELVE
ODES

Addressing Maecenas, his beloved patron, Horace gives examples of the various activities men devote themselves to—chariot racing, politics, cornering the grain supply, farming, trading, repose, soldiering, hunting. But as a skilled poet, Horace feels close to the gods; and unlike other people, his mind is filled with the traditional images of poetry. All this will last for him if only the muses continue their inspiration. And if Maecenas thinks him as a good as the classical poets, his pride will know no bounds.

> *Maecenas atavis edite regibus,*
> *o et praesidium et dulce decus meum,*
> *sunt quos curriculo pulverem Olympicum*
> *collegisse iuvat metaque fervidis*
> *evitata rotis palmaque nobilis*
> *terrarum dominos evehit ad deos.*
> *hunc si mobilium turba Quiritium*
> *certat tergeminos tollere honoribus;*
> *illum si proprio condidit horreo*
> 10   *quicquid de Libycis verritur areis.*
> *guadentem patrios findere sarculo*
> *agros Attalicis condicionibus*
> *numquam demoveas, ut trabe Cypria*
> *Myrtoum pavidus nauta secet mare.*
> *luctantem Icariis fluctibus Africum*
> *mercator metuens otium et oppidi*
> *laudat rura sui; mox reficit rates*
> *quassas, indocilis pauperiem pati.*
> *est qui nec veteris pocula Massici*
> 20   *nec partem solido demere de die*
> *spernit, nunc viridi membra sub arbuto*
> *stratus, nunc ad aquae lene caput sacrae.*
> *multos castra iuvant et lituo tubae*
> *permixtus sonitus bellaque matribus*

TO MAECENAS: HORACE'S CHOICE OF LIFE

Maecenas, scion of the ancient kings,
O my defense and sweet source of my fame,
it pleases some to whirl up Olympic dust
with their chariots, their glowing wheels grazing
the turning posts, whom the palm branch of glory
makes lords of the earth, even one with the gods.
This man likes fickle Roman citizens
to keep on electing him to public office.
That man likes storing up in his granary
all that is swept from Libyan threshing floors.
The fellow who enjoys hoeing the hard dirt
of his family farm will not be lured
by royal Attalic wealth to timidly
sail the Myrtoan sea on a Cyprian bark.
The trader fearful of contending waves
and winds praises the peace and quiet of
his native country-seat; soon he repairs
his damaged ships, unwilling to live on little.
One can't resist cups of old Massic wine
or cutting short his business hours, at times
reclining underneath a green arbutus,
at times by the sacred source of a gentle stream.
Many like army camps and the mingled notes
of military trumpets, which all mothers

detestata. manet sub Iove frigido
venator tenerae coniugis immemor,
seu visa est catulis cerva fidelibus,
seu rupit teretes Marsus aper plagas.
me doctarum hederae praemia frontium
dis miscent superis, me gelidum nemus
Nympharumque leves cum Satyris chori
secernunt populo, si neque tibias
Euterpe cohibet nec Polyhymnia
Lesboum refugit tendere barbiton.
quodsi me lyricis vatibus inseris,
sublimi feriam sidera vertice.

detest. The hunter stays out in the cold
all night, without a thought of his wife's soft charms,
if, say, his trusty hounds have sighted a deer,
or a Marsian boar has pierced his tight nets.
For me, the ivy gracing learned poets'
brows sets me among the gods; and unlike others,
I see the forms of cool groves, lightsome dancing
of Nymphs with Satyrs, so long as Euterpe
does not withhold her flute or Polyhymnia
refuse to stretch the strings of her Lesbian lyre.
And if you rank me with the lyrical bards
of Greece, my lofty head will strike the stars.

Addressing the ship bearing Virgil to Greece, Horace prays for its successful voyage. The dangers of the sea inspire a feeling of rueful wonder at the intrepidity of the first man to brave them and thus violate the evident wish of god. But prohibited dangers are constantly being risked, as show the examples of Prometheus, Daedalus, and Hercules. In fact, by aiming at heaven, we force Jove to punish us.

> *Sic te diva potens Cypri,*
> > *sic fratres Helenae, lucida sidera*
> *vetorumque regat pater*
> > *obstrictis aliis praeter Iapyga,*
> *navis, quae tibi creditum*
> > *debes Vergilium: finibus Atticis*
> *reddas incolumem, precor,*
> > *et serves animae dimidium meae.*
> *illi robur et aes triplex*
> > *circa pectus erat, qui fragilem truci*
> *commisit pelago ratem*
> > *primus, nec timuit praecipitem Africum*
> *decertantem Aquilonibus*
> > *nec tristes Hyadas nec rabiem Noti,*
> *quo non arbiter Hadriae*
> > *maior, tollere seu ponere volt freta.*
> > *quem mortis timuit gradum*
> > *qui siccis oculis monstra natantia,*
> *qui vidit mare turbidum et*
> > *infames scopulos, Acroceraunia?*
> *nequiquam deus abscidit*
> > *prudens Oceano dissociabili*
> *terras, si tamen impiae*
> > *non tangenda rates transiliunt vada.*
> *audax omnia perpeti*
> > *gens humana ruit per vetitum nefas.*

10

20

VIRGIL AND THE DANGERS OF THE SEA

For him may Venus, queen of Cyprus,
    for him may Helen's brothers, those bright stars,
and wind-father Aeolus guide you
    (all other winds except Iapyx confined),
O ship to whom we lent our Virgil
    and who must give him back: to Attic shores
deliver him unharmed, I beg
    of you, and save one-half of my own soul.
Hard oak and triple bronze must he
    have had about his heart who first
sent his frail craft over fierce seas,
    and did not fear Africus' head-long squalls
battling the blasts of Boreas
    or gloomy Hyades or frenzied Notus
(no greater Adriatic ruler,
    whether he wants to raise or still the waves).
What nearing step of Death did he fear
    who dry-eyed stared at swimming monsters,
stared at the wild sea waves, and at those
    infamous cliffs, Acroceraunia?
In vain did god wisely divide
    each land from others by estranging Ocean,
if, even so, impious ships
    skim over traits he did not want crossed.
Audaciously enduring any danger,
    humans rush toward forbidden wrongs.

audax Iapeti genus
    ignem fraude mala gentibus intulit.
post ignem aetheria domo
        subductum macies et nova febrium
        terris incubuit cohors
        semotique prius tarda necessitas
Leti corripuit gradum.
        expertus vacuum Daedalus aëra
pinnis non homini datis;
        perrupit Acheronta Herculeus labor.
nil mortalibus ardui est;
        caelum ipsum petimus stultitia, neque
per nostrum patimur scelus
        iracunda Iovem ponere fulmina.

Audaciously Iapetus' son
    by evil craft brought fire to human beings.
Once fire was stolen from its home
    in heaven, wasting ills and a new troop
of fevers fell upon the earth;
    and, once remote and slowly moving, Death,
always man's doom, quickened its step.
    Daedalus tried to fly through airy space
on wings forbidden to human use;
    Hercules' striving broke through Acheron.
No effort is too arduous
    for mortals; heaven itself we aim at, fools,
and, by our sinning, do not allow
    Jove to lay down his angry thunderbolts.

Horace points out to Sestius the pleasing features of the return of spring. He advises taking advantage of this season, for Death comes soon enough for all, and then life's little pleasures are no long possible.

Solvitur acris hiems grata vice veris et Favoni,
    trahuntque siccas machinae carinas,
ac neque iam stabulis gaudet pecus aut arator igni,
    nec prata canis albicant pruinis.

iam Cytherea choros ducit Venus imminente luna,
    iunctaeque Nymphis Gratiae decentes
alterno terram quatiunt pede, dum graves Cyclopum
    Volcanus ardens visit officinas.

nunc decet aut viridi nitidum caput impedire myrto
10   *aut flore, terrae quem ferunt solutae;*
nunc et in umbrosis Fauno decet immolare lucis,
    seu poscat agna sive malit haedo.

pallida Mors aequo pulsat pede pauperum tabernas
    regumque turres. o beati Sesti,
vitae summa brevis spem nos vetat incohare longam,
    iam te premet nox fabulaeque Manes

et domus exilis Plutonia, quo simul mearis,
    nec regna vini sortiere talis,
nec tenerum Lycidan mirabere, quo calet iuventus
20   *nunc omnis et mox virgines tepebunt.*

SPRING'S INTIMATIONS OF MORTALITY

As welcome Spring and Zephyrs return, hard Winter begins to
melt,
    and winches draw dry hulls down to the sea,
and cattle no longer enjoy their stalls, or plowmen hearthfires,
    and meadows are unblanched by shining hoarfrost.

Now Venus leads off choral dances beneath the bright low moon,
    and hand in hand with the Nymphs, the lovely Graces
one foot after the other strike the ground, while glowing Vulcan
    inspects the Cyclopes' ponderous forges.

Now is the time to wreathe one's glistening brow with verdant myrtle
    or with flowers newly born of the opening earth;
now too, in shady groves, the time to sacrifice to Faunus
    a lamb, or if he prefer it, a kid.

Pale Death pounds at the doors both of the poor man's shack
    and of the rich man's palace. O my Sestius,
blest in all things, life's short season prevents planting high hopes.
    Soon night will afflict you, the storied Shades,

and the bleak halls of Pluto, where, arrived, you will no more
    either cast dice to rule the drinking bout
or gaze with joy on luscious Lycidas, for whom all young men
    now burn, and for whom girls will soon grow warm.

Horace counsels Thaliarchus: in the light of the power of nature and the relative powerlessness of human beings, we should creatively exploit natural pleasures while we can.

Vides ut alta stet nive candidum
Soracte, nec iam sustineant onus
   silvae laborantes, geluque
     flumina constiterint acuto?

dissolve frigus ligna super foco
large reponens atque benignius
   deprome quadrimum Sabina,
     o Thaliarche, merum diota.

permitte divis cetera, qui simul
10   *stravere ventos aequore fervido*
   deproeliantes, nec cupressi
     nec veteres agitantur orni.

quid sit futurum cras, fuge quaerere et
quem Fors dierum cumque dabit, lucro
   appone nec dulces amores
     sperne puer neque tu choreas,

donec virenti canities abest
morosa. nunc et Campus et areae
   lenesque sub noctem susurri
20   *composita repetantur hora,*

TO THALIARCHUS: LIVE NOW

Do you see how Soracte stands glistening
with deep snow, how the straining trees no longer
    sustain the weight, how the rivers
        have frozen still from the sharp cold?

Take off the chill by heaping high more wood
on the hearthfire, and more generously
    pour from its Sabine jar the wine
        of four winters, O Thaliarchus.

Leave to the gods everything else, for once
they have quieted the winds battling each other
    on the angry sea, neither the cypress
        nor the ancient ash is agitated.

Don't worry about what will happen tomorrow,
and count as profit each day Fortune brings,
    and be sure not to scorn, young man,
        sweet loves and dancing in a ring,

while peevish gray age is remote from your
green youth. Now let the Campus and the squares
    and soft whispers in the evening
        be cherished at the appointed hour.

nunc et latentis proditor intumo
gratus puellae risus ab angulo
    pignusque dereptum lacertis
        aut digito male pertinaci.

Now too the pleasing laughter that betrays
the hiding-place of—guess who!—your girl-friend,
    the trophy snatched from her arm or finger,
        as she barely pretends resistance.

Horace advises Leuconoë to give up trying to find out through astrology when they are going to die. Whether they will have long or short lives, it is best simply to take what comes. Right now they should aim at pleasure of the moment; there may not be a tomorrow.

Tu ne quaesieris—scire nefas—quem mihi, quem tibi
finem di dederint, Leuconoë, nec Babylonios
temptaris numeros. ut melius, quicquid erit, pati,
seu plures hiemes, seu tribuit Iuppiter ultimam,
quae nunc oppositis debelitat pumicibus mare
Tyrrhenum. sapias, vina liques, et spatio brevi
spem longam reseces. dum loquimur, fugerit invida
aetas: carpe diem, quam minimum credula postero.

TAKE PLEASURE TODAY

Stop trying to learn what is wrong to know,
the dates assigned by the gods for our deaths,
mine, yours, Leuconoë; don't fool with quack
horoscopes. It makes better sense to endure
whatever happens, no matter if Jove
has destined us to live through other winters,
or only this one as our last, which now
wearies the might of the Tyrrhenian Sea
against the soft, eroded rocks. Be wise:
chill and breathe our wine; prune high hopes to suit
our short season. Even as we speak, unfriendly
time is already stealing away. Take pleasure
today; put only slight trust in tomorrow.

Horace complains to Chloë that she runs away from him like a lost fawn in the wilderness, alarmed by even the most innocent movements of natural things. But, he tells her, he's no ferocious beast that will harm her. Besides, she's a woman now, and must break away from her mother.

Vitas inueleo me similis, Chloë,
quaerenti pavidam montibus aviis
matrem non sine vano
aurarum et silvae metu.

nam seu mobilibus veris inhorruit
adventus foliis, seu virides rubum
dimovere lacertae
et corde et genibus tremit.

atqui non ego te tirgris ut aspera
10 *Gaetulusve leo frangere persequor:*
tandem desine matrem
tempestiva sequi viro.

TO CHLOË: SOME TIMELY ADVICE

Chloë, you're trying to escape me, like
a fawn looking for her timorous mother
    on lonely mountain sides,
        with empty fear of breezes and trees.

If spring's arrival makes the pliant leaves
quiver and rustle, or if through the bushes
    green lizards force their way,
        both in heart and in knees she trembles.

But I'm no fierce tiger or Afric lion
to hunt you down and eat you up—not me!
    Quit clinging to your mother;
        you're grown-up, ready for a man.

Horace tells the courtesan Lydia that young men have begun to lose interest in her. Once she could reject suitors, but when she gets old she will be rejected completely by them; she will be left alone in her house to her lonely lust. Then she will self-pityingly lament the male preference for what is young and fresh.

Parcius iunctas quatiunt fenestras
ictibus crebris iuvenes protervi
nec tibi somnos adimunt, amatque
    ianua limen,

quae prius multum facilis movebat
cardines. audis minus et minus iam:
"me tuo longas pereunte noctes,
    Lydia, dormis?"

invicem moechos anus arrogantes
10   *flebis in solo levis angiportu,*
Thracio bacchante magis sub inter-
    lunia vento,

cum tibi flagrans amor et libido,
quae solet matres furiare equorum,
saeviet circa iecur ulcerosum,
    non sine questu,

laeta quod pubes hedera virenti
gaudeat pulla magis atque myrto,
aridas frondes hiemis sodali
20   *dedicet Euro.*

TO LYDIA: THINGS WILL GET EVEN WORSE

Less frequently do your barred shutters clatter
from stones tossed up by impudent young men,
nor do they rob you of sleep, and your door
        sticks to its threshold,

though once it would swing open easily
on warm hinges. You hear less often now:
"While I languish, how can you, Lydia,
        sleep through the long nights?"

You'll pay when old; then scornful fornicators
will makes you cry, left in your lonely alley,
while the cold Thracian wind raves in the inter-
lunary darkness,

and in your heart the flaming lust and longing
which is wont to madden the mothers of horses
will rampage through your lacerated flesh and
        bring some complaining

that lusty males delight in fresh green ivy
and rich dark myrtle wreathes, but dedicate
all withered garlands to the blasts of Eurus,
        partner of winter.

Horace calls upon his friends to celebrate, now that the Egyptian queen has committed suicide. Up to now, though defeated at Actium, she was stil dangerous, deluded by wine and by a degenerate court. But Caesar's keen pursuit helped waken her to reality. Still, her remarkable courage at the end showed that she was, finally, truly noble.

Nunc est bibendum, nunc pede libero
pulsanda tellus, nunc Saliaribus
 ornare pulvinar deorum
  tempus erat dapibus, sodales.

antehac nefas depromere Caecubum
cellis avitis, dum Capitolio
 regina dementes ruinas,
  funus et imperio parabat

contaminato cum grege turpium
10 *morbo virorum, quidlebet impotens*
 sperare fortunaque dulci
  ebria, sed minuit furorem

vix una sospes navis ab ignibus,
mentemque lymphatam Mareotico
 redegit in veros timores
  Caesar, ab Italia volantem

remis adurgens, accipiter velut
molles columbas aut leporem citus
 venator in campis nivalis
20 *Haemoniae, daret ut catenis*

THE DOOM OF CLEOPATRA

Now we should drink, now unrestrainedly
dance to the beat; now would be time to honor
    our imaged gods with cultic feasts
        of Salian luxury, my friends.

Before this day it would have been wrong to pour
our fathers' Caecuban, while she, the queen,
    planned mad ruin for the Capitol
        and the demise of Roman rule,

with her polluted flock of "males," each one
perversely foul. Indulgently, she hoped
    for everything, drunk on the flattery
        of Fortune. But her frenzy lessened

when scarcely one ship came safe from the fire.
Her mind, deluded by Egyptian wine,
    was taught justified fear by Caesar,
        when in her flight from Italy

he pressed after her closely (as a hawk
a delicate dove or a speedy hunter
    a hare over the snowy plains
        of Thessaly) to bind in chains

fatale monstrum. quae generosius
perire quaerens nec muliebriter
 expavit ensem nec latentes
  classe cita reparavit oras.

ausa et iacentem visere regiam
vultu sereno, fortis et asperas
 tractare serpentes, ut atrum
  corpore combiberet venenum,

deliberata morte ferocior;
saevis Liburnis scilicet invidens
 privata deduci superbo
  non humilis mulier triumpho.

this fatal, monstrous being. But she, seeking
nobly to die, neither effeminately
    dreaded the sword nor tried to escape
        in her swift ship to obscure lands.

Strong was her spirit as she gazed serenely
at the impotent royal precincts; brave, as she
    took up those cruel snakes to drink
        with her body the deadly venom;

fiercer for her resolve to die, refusing
of course a rough return, no longer royal,
    on enemy ships to their proud
        triumph—a not ignoble woman.

Horace tells Barine he can't believe a word she says, since not only do her lies to lovers go unpunished by the gods, but each perjury seems to bring her new beauty. What's more, the divinities of love, who should punish her crimes, are merely amused by her. So each new generation of men enslaves itself permanently to her, while parents fear her, and especially new brides, who see her leading their husbands astray.

Ulla si iuris tibi peierati
poena, Barine, nocuisset umquam,
dente si negro fieres vel uno
      turpior ungui,

crederem. sed tu simul obligasti
perfidum votis caput, enitescis
pulchrior multo iuvenumque prodis
      publica cura.

expedit matris cineres opertos
10   *fallere et toto taciturna noctis*
signa cum caelo gelidaque divos
      morte carentes.

ridet hoc, inquam, Venus ipsa; rident
simplices Nymphae ferus et Cupido,
semper ardentis acuens sagittas
      cote cruenta.

adde quod pubes tibi crescit omnis,
servitus crescit nova, nec priores
impiae tectum dominae relinquunt,
20   *saepe minati.*

TO PERFIDIOUS BUT BEAUTIFUL BARINE

If perjured promises had ever brought you
even the slightest punishment, Barine,
if the least spot on tooth or fingernail
    blemished your beauty,

I might believe you now. But when you vow
lyingly on your life, you start to glow,
lovelier than before, becoming youth's
    favorite female.

You've made it pay to swear falsely by the ashes
of your mother, the silent constellations,
the entire sky, and the gods who never know
    death and its coldness.

Even Venus laughs at this, the artless Nymphs
laugh, and so too cruel Cupid, always honing
his fiery arrows on a whetstone all
    dripping with heart's blood.

Besides, all our young men grow up for you—
your latest band of slaves, their predecessors
not leaving their ungodly mistress' house, though
    often they threaten.

te suis matres metuunt iuvencis,
te senes parci miseraeque, nuper
virgines, nuptae, tua ne retardet
aura maritos.

You it is mothers fear for their sons' sake;
you tight old men fear; and sad young brides, too,
lest their new husbands should linger near your
    radiant beauty.

Horace reminds his friend that nothing can stay the swift course of time that leads to old age and death—not virtue, not sacrifices to the gods. We shall all have to exchange life's pleasures for the dreary scenery of Hades' realm.

Eheu fugaces, Postume, Postume,
labunter anni, nec pietas moram
    rugis et instanti senectae
        adferet indomitaeque morti;

non si trecenis quotquot eunt dies,
amice, places inlacrimabilem
    Plutona tauris, qui ter amplum
        Geryonen Tityonque tristi

compescit unda, scilicet omnibus,
10 *quicumque terrae munere vescimur,*
    enaviganda, sive reges
        sive inopes erimus coloni.

frustra cruento Marte carebimus
fractisque rauci fluctibus Hadriae,
    frustra per autumnos nocentem
        corporibus metuemus Austrum.

visendus ater flumine languido
Cocytos errans et Danai genus
    infame damnatusque longi
20   *Sisyphus Aeolides laboris.*

THERE IS NO WAY . . .

Ah, swiftly flow our years, gliding away—
my friend, dear friend—nor will integrity
    delay wrinkles, insistent old
        age, and indomitable Death.

No, not if you tried, with three hundred bulls
offered each day, to soften iron-hearted
    Pluto, who keeps the huge, three-bodied
        Geryon and Tityus confined

beyond the mournful stream that all, yes all
of us who feed on the fruits of this earth,
    must cross, whether the princely rich
        or but the hired, rural poor.

In vain shall we escape bloodthirsty Mars
and the rough waves of roaring Adriatic;
    in vain in autumn shall we guard
        our health from the harmful Sirocco.

Still must we view the winding, languid flow
of dark Cocytus, and the infamous
    Danaan daughters, and Aeolidan
        Sisyphus doomed to unending toil.

linquenda tellus et domus et placens
uxor, neque harum quas colis arborum
    te praeter invisas cupressos
        ulla brevem dominum sequetur.

absumet heres Caecuba dignior
servata centum clavibus et mero
    tinguet pavimentum superbo,
        pontificum potiore cenis.

Still must we leave behind lands, home, and charming
wife, nor will any of the trees you tended
  (except, of course, the hateful cypress)
   follow their soon withering master.

Your worthier heir will drain your Caecuban,
now locked up with one hundred keys, and stain
  your tiled floor with that haughty wine,
  choicer than wine at priestly banquets.

Horace tells Grosphus that all humans desire peace of mind, which cannot be bought, but can be achieved by restricting our desires and cultivating contentment.

Otium divos rogat in patenti
prensus Aegaeo, simul atra nubes
condidit lunam neque certa fulgent
    sidera nautis;

otium bello furiosa Thrace,
otium Medi pharetra decori,
Grosphe, non gemmis neque purpura ve-
    nale neque auro.

non enim gazae neque consularis
summovet lictor miseros tumultus
mentis et curas laqueata circum
    tecta volantes.

vivitur parvo bene cui paternum
splendet in mensa tenui salinum
nec leves somnos timor aut cupido
    sordidus aufert.

quid brevi fortes iaculamur aevo
multa? quid terras alio calentes
sole mutamus? patriae quis exsul
    se quoque fugit?

10

20

TO GROSPHUS: PEACE OF MIND IS BEST

It's peace of mind the person caught in mid-
Aegaean prays for to the gods, when clouds
darken the moon, and when no sailors' stars are
      steadily shining.

For peace of mind even Thrace wild in war,
for peace of mind Medes graced with quivers pray,
peace which, Grosphus, by gems, rich fabrics, or gold
      cannot be purchased.

For not by royal treasure or consular
lictor can we dispel unhappy tumult
of mind or anxious thoughts that swarm beneath
      glittering ceilings.

A man lives well on little where the silver
at modest meals is the paternal salt-dish,
where there's no fear or sordid greed to hinder
      slumbering gently.

Life so brief, why do we eagerly aim at
so much? Why do we trade our home for lands
warmed by an alien sun? What exile ever
      fled from himself, too?

scandit aeratas vitiosa naves
cura nec turmas equitum relinquit
ocior cervis et agente nimbos
    ocior Euro.

laetus in praesens animus quod ultra est
oderit curare et amara lento
temperet risu. nihil est ab omni
    parte beatum.

abstulit clarum cita Mors Achillem,
30   longa Tithonum minuit Senectus;
et mihi forsan tibi quod negarit
    porriget hora.

te greges centum Siculaeque circum
mugiunt vaccae, tibi tollit hinnitum
apta quadrisis equa, te bis Afro
    murice tinctae

vestiunt lanae; mihi parva rura et
spiritum Graiae tenuem Camenae
Parca non mendax dedit et malignum
40   spernere vulgus.

Morbid concern boards even brass-bound yachts
and is never left behind by troops of horse;
it speeds faster than stags and faster than
storm-driving Eurus.

A mind contented with its state disdains
worry about the future, and can temper
afflictions with a calm smile. Happiness
      never is perfect.

Hastening Death cut off glorious Achilles;
lingering Old Age withered away Tithonus;
perhaps what Time denies to you, it will
      offer to Horace.

Surrounding you a hundred herds of cows
from Sicily moo; for you the fine mare
made for the chariot whinnies; you in wool
      twice-dipped in purple

from Africa are dressed. Unlying Fate gives
me but a humble farm, slight inspiration
from the Grecian Muse, and sheer contempt for the
      envious rabble.

At Venus' shrine, Horace formalizes the end of his service to love by dedicating to the goddess the tools of his trade—his lyre and his "weapons." He has one last request: let Chloë pay for what she did to him.

Vixi puellis nuper idoneus
et militavi non sine gloria;
    nunc arma defunctumque bello
       barbiton hic paries habebit,

laevum marinae qui Veneris latus
custodit, hic, hic ponite lucida
    funalia et vectes securesque
       oppositis foribus minaces.

o quae beatum diva tenes Cyprum et
10   *Memphin carentem Sithonia nive,*
    regina, sublimi flagello
       tange Chloën semel arrogantem.

FAREWELL TO LOVE, WITH ONE LAST REQUEST

I've been a ladies' man till recently,
served in the wars of love, not without glory;
    but now my arms and lyre, released
        from service, will adorn this wall,

which from the left guards sea-born Venus' side.
Come, come, boys, offer up here my once brilliant
    torches, my crow-bars, and my axes
        designed for breaking down locked doors.

O goddess ruling rich Cypress and Memphis
free from Sithonian snow, please, queen,
    raise your lash and give just one cut
        to Chloë, arrogant female?

Leonard Moskovit is Professor of English at the University of Colorado, Boulder, where he has taught for 21 years. He has published articles or reviews on Maugham, Dryden, Pope and Horace in journals such as *Studies in Philology*. Recently he has been working on problems of usage, writing, and rhetoric.

Quintus Horatius Flaccus (65 – 8 B.C.), the Roman poet commonly referred to as Horace, was a contemporary of the epic poet Virgil and the emperor Augustus. He published epodes, satires, epistles, and odes, from which these odes were selected.

Romans apparently had knowledge of the magic of the Rowan Tree. Pliny tells us that he knows from his own experience that if a snake be confined within a circle composed in part of fire and in part of branches of the Ash (Rowan), it will escape across the fire rather than touch the Ash. "It is," he goes on, "a wonderful courtesy of nature that the Ash should flower before the serpents appear and not cast its leaves before they are gone again" (i.e. into hibernation).

This book was set in Palatino Medium by e.d. Typesetting in Boston, Massachusetts. The text was printed on acid-free paper by Evans Printing Company in Concord, New Hampshire.

Rowan Tree Press
124 Chestnut Street
Boston, Massachusetts 02108

Poetics and Poetry

THE EIGHT STAGES OF TRANSLATION, Robert Bly
AGAINST OUR VANISHING, Allen Grossman

LOST GOODS & STRAY BEASTS, Peter Sharpe
GREEN MOUNTAIN, BLACK MOUNTAIN, Anne Stevenson
1843 REBECCA 1847, Abbot Cutler
THE JUSTICE-WORM, Nadya Aisenberg
STRIPPING THE TREES, Harris Collingwood
SAINTS, Jean Pedrick

Rowan Tree Press
124 Chestnut Street
Boston, Massachusetts 02108